PICKLE JAR

by Maddie Rice

samuelfrench.co.uk

ISBN 978-0-573-11587-5

www.samuelfrench.co.uk
www.samuelfrench.com

For Amateur Production Enquiries

United Kingdom and World
excluding North America
plays@samuelfrench.co.uk
020 7255 4302/01

Each title is subject to availability from Samuel French, depending upon country of performance.

THINKING ABOUT PERFORMING A SHOW?

There are thousands of plays and musicals available to perform from Samuel French right now, and applying for a licence is easier and more affordable than you might think

---

From classic plays to brand new musicals, from monologues to epic dramas, there are shows for everyone.

Plays and musicals are protected by copyright law, so if you want to perform them, the first thing you'll need is a licence. This simple process helps support the playwright by ensuring they get paid for their work and means that you'll have the documents you need to stage the show in public.

Not all our shows are available to perform all the time, so it's important to check and apply for a licence before you start rehearsals or commit to doing the show.

LEARN MORE & FIND THOUSANDS OF SHOWS

Browse our full range of plays and musicals, and find out more about how to license a show

www.samuelfrench.co.uk/perform

Talk to the friendly experts in our Licensing team for advice on choosing a show and help with licensing

plays@samuelfrench.co.uk   020 7387 9373

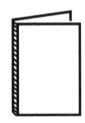

MUSIC USE NOTE

Licensees are solely responsible for obtaining formal written permission from copyright owners to use copyrighted music in the performance of this play and are strongly cautioned to do so. If no such permission is obtained by the licensee, then the licensee must use only original music that the licensee owns and controls. Licensees are solely responsible and liable for all music clearances and shall indemnify the copyright owners of the play(s) and their licensing agent, Samuel French, against any costs, expenses, losses and liabilities arising from the use of music by licensees. Please contact the appropriate music licensing authority in your territory for the rights to any incidental music.

USE OF COPYRIGHT MUSIC

A licence issued by Samuel French Ltd to perform this play does not include permission to use the incidental music specified in this copy.

Where the place of performance is already licensed by the PERFORMING RIGHT SOCIETY (PRS) a return of the music used must be made to them. If the place of performance is not so licensed then application should be made to the PRS, 2 Pancras Square, London, N1C 4AG.

A separate and additional licence from PHONOGRAPHIC PERFORMANCE LTD, 1 Upper James Street, London W1F 9DE (www.ppluk.com) is needed whenever commercial recordings are used.

IMPORTANT BILLING AND CREDIT REQUIREMENTS

If you have obtained performance rights to this title, please refer to your licensing agreement for important billing and credit requirements.

ABOUT THE AUTHOR

Maddie is an actress and writer.

As a writer, she has worked with Soho Theatre Writers' Lab. *Handy*, a sitcom she wrote in collaboration with Kate Kennedy, is currently being made into a pilot by RTE.

As an actress she has performed in *Fleabag* (Soho Theatre/UK/ AUS tour), *Villain* (King's Head Theatre), *All My Sons* (Regents Park Theatre), *Henry V* (West End), *Every Blank Ever, I Live with Models* (Comedy Central), *Who Killed Laura Kitchens?*, *Call the Midwife* (BBC).

She also writes and performs as a member of comedy groups zazU and Lead Pencil.

AUTHOR'S NOTE

Pickle Jar is a story created by its characters. I didn't set out to write a play exploring these themes and the eventual story emerged before the subjects became commonplace in current affairs.

I began by writing down stories that I found funny or emotive and the world and its characters grew out of these.

I was always fascinated by responsibility and our society's perceptions of culpability and blame, especially relating to people in public service – hence my choice to make MISS a teacher.

At the time I had also been thinking a lot about how people, in particular women, would often rather blame themselves than others, especially when it relates to sexual or romantic conduct. I think this is an interesting character trait to explore as, while it can be damaging, it comes from an empathetic need to see people as good.

Humour is a useful tool in storytelling and coping with what life throws at us, and I've tried to reflect that in this play and the way MISS makes her way through it. Enjoy!

Maddie Rice
July 2018

Pickle Jar was first presented by Fight in the Dog and United Agents at the Underbelly, Edinburgh Fringe on 2 August 2018.

CAST

MISS – Maddie Rice

Voices by Dave Bibby and the students of Musical Youth London.

Directed and Developed by Katie Pesskin
Set and Costume Design by Alice Hallifax
Sound Design by Ciaran Clarke
Lighting Design by Mark Dymock
Stage Managed by Russell Rosewood

Front cover photography by Amelia J Dowd
Front cover artwork by Anneliese Nappa

CHARACTER

MISS – the narrator. A teacher in her late twenties.

This was originally written and performed as a play for one actress.

The other characters can be played by the actress playing MISS, played by other actors or recorded as voice overs.

SCRIPT NOTES

[ ]   Text in square brackets is something that is thought but not said.
–   Dashes indicate an unfinished thought.
/   Slashes indicate an interruption.
Speech in bold is directed at the audience.

The setting for this play should be somewhat abstract and reflect the emotional state of the narrator.

This text went to print in rehearsals and may differ from what made it to the first performance.

ACKNOWLEDGEMENTS

Katie Pesskin for her constant ideas, encouragement and belief-

Thank you for making this with me.

Alex Pritchett, for getting me started, without you this wouldn't exist. Nicola Kill and Mimi Edwards for your endless talent and vital help with workshopping. My friends, especially Megan Folley, for your teacher stories and support. My incredibly supportive and wonderful family. Big thanks to Brid Kirby, Miriam Attwood, Mim Black, Charlotte Bennett and everyone at Soho Theatre Writers' Lab, Alex Turner, Olivia Emden, Katharine Armitage, Tom Machell, Phoebe Waller-Bridge, Vicky Jones, Francesca Moody, David Luff, Louise Carter, Timo Willman, Musical Youth London students, Dave Bibby, Gabriel Bisset-Smith, Jess MacDonald, Naomi MacDonald, The Cockpit Theatre 'New Stuff' Night, Stephanie Moore, Katya Balfour-Lynn, Frances Greenfield and Olivia Jones at United Agents, Jessica Francis, Aileen McEwan, James Penford and George Ward at Hatton McEwan Penford, The Peggy Ramsey Foundation, Duncan Hayes, David Johnson and John Mackay.

A huge thank you to everyone who donated to the Fringe Funder for Edinburgh Fringe 2018: Lucy Mcginn, Bob Hirst, Chloe Taylor, Jonathan Derry-Evans, Lorenzo Levrini, Tom Downey, Owen Pugh, Thomas Coombes, Caoimhe Kirby, Sarah Robson, Toby Mountford, Tom Levinge, Dave Bibby, Deirdre Garvey, Jonathan Mellor, Peter McGladdery, Lex Slater, Madalena Hudson, Toni Ryan, Ricky Johnston, Tessa Rice, Mary Duggan, Pippa Kelly, Amelia Rice, Brendan Fenerty, Jonny Moore, Ste Montgomery, Ali Dowling, Kirsty Mann, Jenny Tozer, Jane Markwell, Catherine Garratt, Sarah Crosbie, Ilona Village, Charles Miller, Francesca Moody, Peadar Kirby, Eloise Akehurst, Philippa Massouh, AJ Fleet, John Rice, Claudia Newland, Tom Machell, Marcus Rice and Sophie Hawes.

For Katie

Very dramatic thriller music plays.

Stark light comes up in a spotlight on a woman. She is terrified.

MISS Do I know you?

I'm sure you are very nice but I don't know you, do I?

Are you looking for directions or something?

I'm in a hurry to get home.

Can you back off, please?

No. No.

MISS *acts as if someone is trying to kiss her.*

Get off!

I said no.

I am calling the police. Right now!

She backs away.

Trust you? No. I don't trust you because you are a stranger. A complete stranger!

Leave me alone! Get away from me! Leave me ALONE!

She falls to the ground as if she has been pushed and lies dead on the floor.

Beat.

She jumps up enthusiastically, suddenly out of character.

The lights change. We are in the classroom. She takes out her phone, taps it and the thriller music cuts.

Ok. So, girls, what do we think was the message of that?

Come on? This is meant to be fun. I was trying to make it come off the page a bit more.

Any questions?

Not one question?

You can ask me anything. Anything you like.

Yes. Finally. A hand. Thank you, Carly.

CARLY Do you have a boyfriend, Miss?

MISS Carly Hancock! How is that relevant?

CARLY You said we could ask anything, Miss.

MISS Very funny. And how does whether I have a – a partner or not matter to form time?

CARLY Well, if you aren't getting any then we have to deal with the stress.

The GIRLS *fall about laughing.*

MISS ...Alright then, if you want to talk about boyfriends so much then maybe we could do the next session on love and we could all read out love poems we've written?

The GIRLS *groan.*

Didn't think so.

Can anyone tell me what today's PSHE was about?

Please!

GEMMA Stranger danger.

MISS Thank you, Gemma. We got there in the end.

Stranger danger. Trust *no one*!

No, I'm joking.

I know this may sound trivial to you girls but after what happened in the village with the man...with his...

I think it's worth talking about/

CARLY *(pointing at the window)* /Look, Miss! A stranger.

MISS What? Oh, Carly. That's Mr Ellis.

The GIRLS *chant and whistle.*

V/O GIRLS Stranger danger! Stranger danger!

MISS Girls, stop. Claire. Sit down. Rachel. No. Girls! Hang on. Sorry, Jack.

MISS *opens the window.*

MISS Girls! Enough!

MISS *sticks her head out the window.*

Sorry. What were you saying?

MR ELLIS Umm – I – I like your cardigan.

MISS Oh. Thank you. It's – uh – it's reversible.

Was that all?

MR ELLIS Yeah. Sorry. I wasn't actually expecting you to open the window.

Hiya, girls.

MISS Sorry about this, Mr Ellis, everyone is a bit excitable today. I'll see you in the staffroom.

She closes the window.

Right, where were we?

GEMMA Nice cardigan, Miss!

Beat.

(MISS *addressing the audience*)
Yes. I was wearing this cardigan.

I need to dress like a teacher. Because I am a teacher!

Anyway, it's not a *cardigan* cardigan. It doesn't do up and it's long and it's not from M&S. So...

I like it, to be honest. I'm wearing it now and I'm not teaching, am I?

There really isn't anything wrong with it!

Sorry. I don't know why I'm being so... It's...

I've been sitting up on the mound opposite the school for ages. I've bought a tree and I need to find a place to/

MISS*'s phone rings. It is a song by Justin Bieber*.*

Mairead.

Not now, Mairead.

She cancels the call and puts her phone away.

The kids love that song.

Mairead's my housemate. We met teaching at Lincoln Hill and we've lived together ever since. She's mad. She goes *out* out on weeknights.

MAIREAD You need to go out on Wednesdays! It's electric. I got fingered in the smoking area of Spoons.

MISS Ew, Mairead!

MAIREAD What? People don't do it enough anymore! It made me feel really young!

I've no idea how old she is. She's celebrated her twenty-first birthday every year I've known her and she dresses like a teenager.

MAIREAD Lost property win! I'm a unicorn queen!

She's my best friend at school and in the world too.

Well, school is my world.

I teach English and I'm a form tutor. I have to do PSHE lessons on stuff they clearly already know about. Stranger danger, sex ed, friendships. I once did a session on the

---

* */** A licence to produce *Pickle Jar* does not include a performance licence to play a Justin Bieber song. For further information, please see Music Use Note on page v.

dangers of the internet and the only way I could think to dramatise the session was to act like a porn star.

So I decided to just put an episode of *Catfish* on the projector.

MISS So you see, girls, you could be talking to anyone. Anyone can get hold of a picture of Justin Bieber.

CARLY D'ya like Justin Bieber, Miss?

MISS No! I mean, yes. He's very talented, Carly. I thought that's who you liked?

CARLY No way, Miss. He's a boy. We like men.

MISS What? No. You like boys your own age.

Ok, look, we've nearly run out of time. The important thing is that you change your privacy settings on all these social media apps to private, so people have to add you and they don't find out where you live and type it into their Google Maps and follow you home and just... Kill you. Ok?

CARLY Yours isn't private, Miss.

MISS Yes, it is.

The OTHER GIRLS *laugh.*

CARLY Nope. Not on Instagram. Look, here she is.

Eighteen followers. Congrats, Miss, good for you! Hashtag marking, hashtag face mask, hashtag single but ain't got time to mingle, hashtag/

MISS /Ok! Yes. Thank you. That...is unfortunate. It's better to be private. I'll be changing mine at lunch.

CARLY Worried you'll get too many followers, Miss?

Carly Hancock. She's smart. Not smarter than me but she's really clever.

Sometimes I used to walk down the corridor and pretend I was her. It made me feel powerful and confident.

I realise how stupid that sounds.

Sorry.

Where was I?

Oh yeah. I was trying to buy this tree on the internet.

Which sounds easy but I didn't know exactly what I wanted. You're supposed to buy the tree and the labourer to plant the tree and declare where you are planting it.

I don't know why they make it so hard. By planting a tree I am literally adding oxygen to the air, saving the planet and helping people not to die.

I need to get out more. Mairead's always having a go at me about it. She tells me a lot about myself. Mainly in the form of made-up analogies.

MAIREAD You know what you are? You are like a clam.

   A little closed fucking clam. Open it up.

   Go out. Open your shell. Polish your little pearl. And let some people fucking touch it!

She thinks I'm a prude.

I'm not a prude.

I just don't like to...

She says I can't even say the word sex but there, I just said it.

I always try and tell Mairead my sex stories, what I did with my ex, but she just laughs.

Seb. My last boyfriend.

We met at a friend of mine's engagement party. He made me laugh so hard I choked on a canapé and spat it all over his face. He looked at me, wiped the salmon blini off his forehead, gave me a new one and kissed me.

And I couldn't believe it because I looked disgusting and I'd just been telling him the most boring story about a wind turbine changing direction.

But after that we were just – it felt so easy. There were no games or holding back.

We were really honest about how much we fancied each other. Or, well, he was. I just thought really hard about telling him I loved him and spent ages thinking of ways of doing it so I didn't have to be there when it happened.

Then, one night, I cooked him a romantic dinner. Candles all around the room. I was wearing a red dress and an uncomfortable sexy, strappy bodice that meant I couldn't sit down.

But I felt courageous in it. Courageous enough to tell him. I love you.

I was trying to work out how I would eat standing up, I thought I maybe we could have sex before dinner and then I could just pop on some comfies. But then it was half eight and he wasn't there.

I rang him. Text him. Undid a few of the straps.

Ten. He still wasn't there.

I left him a load of messages. Checked his Facebook. Nothing.

And I just knew.

I googled traffic accidents in the area. There had been a big crash on the A-road that he might have used on his bike.

We were quite new so I hadn't met his parents, or any of his friends yet. They wouldn't know to tell me – to contact me if something had happened. Not invited to my own boyfriend's funeral.

My phone rang at midnight. His number. Someone must have found him on the road and called me. His last missed call.

MISS What's happened? Hello?

SEB Hey, babycakes!

MISS Seb? Seb! You're alive!

SEB Yeah. I need to tell you something.

MISS Me too.

SEB I've got something.

MISS Seb. We said no presents! You didn't have to get/

SEB /No. Umm, listen. I've just been tested and the doctors said that I have the signs of an STI. I've got this thing, like a man's cystitis. It's a sort of... chlamydia.

MISS Oh. Haha. What?

SEB I'm really sorry, babe. Doctor said it's normally sexually transmitted but I could have got it from a dirty towel. So, I don't know whether you've given it to me, or I've given it to you or whatever, but you need to get tested.

MISS Oh, yeah. Cool. I will. Should anyway really. That is so funny. Are you ok?

SEB Yup, I'm fine. I mean, this isn't making my day, and obviously I am going to have to call a couple of other people.

MISS Oh. Ok. Cool. Yeah – me too, gonna have to – yeah.

SEB Do you hate me? You should hate me.

MISS No, no way. I don't hate you, I – everyone has STIs.

SEB Umm, not everyone but yeah, thanks for being so cool about it.

MISS Of course. Are you still coming over?

SEB Umm, yeah, I've been thinking/

MISS Yeah, me too, I/

SEB /It's all been getting a bit serious, so maybe we/

MISS We should keep it casual?

SEB /should just be friends, babe, yeah? Anyway, better go.

MISS I—

He hangs up.

It's ok.

It was a very casual, casual thing.

Casual, in that he was casual and I – wanted to marry him.

But I'm over it now, it's been nearly six months and I only ever check his Instagram if I'm feeling really shit about myself.

He could be so sweet. He wrote me a poem on a napkin, took me to Winter Wonderland and he named a character in one of his animations after me.

It was a fat fish who couldn't swim but he was one of those underdog heroes.

When we broke up Mairead made me ritually burn some socks he'd left at mine. She is a great friend.

Last night, we were having a TV dinner night to cheer me up but we don't have a TV so we watched *Notting Hill* on her iPad.

I was eating a cheesy pasta medley I'd made with all the leftover pasta I could find in the cupboard. Mairead's on this diet where she only eats orange foods. Carrots, tomato soup, sweet potato. Last night she was eating a bag of Wotsits.

MAIREAD I found a loophole.

She'd drunk an entire bottle of Cabernet Sauvignon and wine is like truth serum to her so I knew she was going to have a go about house stuff. We'd run out of pretty much everything and it was my turn so I knew I should let her have the last word but –

MISS Cabernet Sauvignon isn't orange.

MAIREAD Oh fuck off. What are you, the food police? I didn't have a go at you for mixing three different types of pasta shapes in a bowl. It was giving me a migraine. Make a choice.

I don't want to argue. Just talk to me. I know you're finding it hard.

I stormed off to my room and found a meditation tape on YouTube to calm me down. It made me imagine myself walking through a forest and smelling the cool air and I imagined my tree in the forest.

We used to do meditation at school. Miss Sanchez, the Spanish teacher, taught yoga classes once a week in the Great Hall. Don't get excited by the name, it was just the canteen with the benches pushed to the side.

Miss Sanchez is very spiritual. She claims to be a psychic! Once, she accosted Mr Peters in the corridor to tell him:

MISS SANCHEZ Your dog is in peril. Very, very sick. I sensed this.

Go, go, save your doggy.

Mr Peters didn't have a dog. But she once felt my leg in cobra pose and said she could sense that I didn't have a father figure in my life which...which I never told her so she must be a bit psychic.

So yoga's every Friday before school. It's where Mairead and I go to gossip.

The day I told her I'd fucked it with Seb she said:

MAIREAD Are you kidding? He fucked it with you! I tell you what, if I see him again I am going to rip out his spine because you cannot act like a spineless shit if you want to keep your spine.

MISS Thank you.

MAIREAD You know what you need? You need to get under someone else. And I'm talking about real sex with a stranger up against a skip in the road.

It's like rollerblading, ye know? Getting back on the blades after you've gone down some stairs. Having wheels on your feet is fun but maybe roll down a slide next time or a small tuffet. Change it up. Don't stop doing it!

D'ye get me?

MISS *is distracted, watching someone in the yoga room.*

MISS Yeah. I just...

MAIREAD Oi! You're checking out Jack Ellis's arse. You little
pervert.

I wasn't. Mr Ellis, the food tech teacher. The one from the
window who said he liked my cardigan.

All the girls fancied him. I didn't really get it.

I mean, he's impossibly tall and muscly and when you look at
him you can imagine him bringing you flowers, fending off
burglars and building Ikea flat-packs without the instructions.

Mairead knew I liked him which I hated because I never
told her and it further proved that she knew me better than
I know myself.

MAIREAD *(rolling up her yoga mat)* Let's go out tonight? Jack,
are you in? Drink some really sugary shit and dance 'til
we die?

MR ELLIS If I dance people might actually die. Seriously. My
limbs do what they want and there could be some casualties.

I laughed way too hard at that. I laughed so hard I started
sweating.

MAIREAD Right, that's sorted then! See you two pricks later.

It's time for this bitch to go and teach some kids about the
Old Testament.

The kids adore her because she swears when she talks about
Jesus. She doesn't even have to try.

Some of the girls think I'm cool. They tease me, like I'm one
of them. Like Carly. She once said I dressed like a jumble
sale on acid.

And they all shop in vintage markets. So that is a compliment.
I think.

(Beat)

Last night after mine and Mairead's argument I couldn't sleep
so I spent the night on the internet. I've become addicted to

looking at my hairdresser Becky's brother's yoga teacher's friend Helen on Instagram. She's so together and pretty and happy and she has a dog and a husband and a marble phone case.

I didn't sleep at all but I found a funeral parlour in Guildford that actually advises you what kind of memorial tree would suit the deceased. There's a questionnaire and you have to book an appointment to find out the result.

Text sound.

Sorry. That's mine.

Laura Warren.

Reading text message aloud.

MISS   "Are you ok? Do you want to talk? I have a Japanese Tabata class but I can skip it."

Ugh. She's the school counsellor. She used to hang around after yoga trying to join our gang. She was desperate for Mairead to like her.

When they first met she said:

LAURA   Mairead, that's such a nice name.

And Mairead just said:

MAIREAD   No.

She is really uptight and uppity and into yoghurt-y vegan-y seedy things. We call her Wet Warren. Me and Mairead. She's rude. Or, well, when she talks to me she always made me feel a bit – not sad but a bit – shit.

Once she cornered me in the stationery cupboard –

LAURA   You seem stressed. Have you ever tried mindfully eating a raisin?

MISS   Umm. No.

LAURA   Oh, you should. It's so great. It's all about living in the moment. You take one raisin. Feel it between your fingers, really experience it there. Then you smell the raisin, roll it around on your lips. Pop it on your tongue, but don't eat it! First you close your eyes. Shake it around in your mouth. Then bite into the raisin, taste the raisin and then you eat it. Ok? Hope that helps.

Obviously I didn't try.

Ok, I did but I was feeling really stressed that day.

Anyway, I put the raisin in my mouth and before I could be mindful I choked on it and it just slipped right down my throat.

Carly had sessions with her. Wet Warren used to laud it over me like I was a bad form tutor.

I imagined them talking about me. Laughing about me together.

I had really awful teachers at school except for Mrs Carter, who was my English teacher, and look where I am now. I just wanted the girls to see me as their Mrs Carter. When I was at school she used to do dance sessions with us that helped us learn about team work.

One PSHE I got my girls to make up dance routines to a song of their choice that represented team work and feminism.

MISS   Ok, girls! Who's showing first? Ok, great, Gemma's group. Off you go.

> GEMMA *strikes a pose. Checks the girls in her group are ready.*

GEMMA   Play.

> *The music plays. The dance is ludicrously sexual.*

> MISS *watches the dance. It gets worse and worse until she turns off the music on her phone.*

MISS   Stop! No. Stop.

GEMMA   *(coming up from a "slut drop")* Oh, Miss!

It was horrible. And fascinating. They do sexy dancing better than any adult I've ever met. It scares me. How mature they all seem.

I secretly spent hours practising what I remembered of Gemma's routine in the mirror. I knew it was unbelievably degrading but it made me feel alive. Imagining having the confidence to do it in public. Imagining I was... [Carly.]

I once got called into the headmaster's office because the school disco ended in an "erotic dance off" and one of the girls told the chaperone that I'd taught them the routine.

The Headmaster at Lincoln is a man called Kim Butterman. I think he's how I imagine God to look.

Mairead calls him a DILF but he doesn't have kids.

He introduced himself to me as:

MR BUTTERMAN   Kim. I know it's a woman's name but my surname is Butterman so just remember it as Kim but a man.

And I did remember.

I saw him loads of times. His old red sofa was spilling stuffing out of the seams from all our meetings.

The day after I broke up with Seb, he made me a hot Ribena to make me feel better. I was in his office talking about a fight between two of my girls:

MISS   Girls! What are you doing? Enough! Come on. Now. Carly. Off. Get off. Gemma, get back please. What are you two girls doing?

Ok, Gemma, are you ok? Let's get a plaster on that. Yes, thank you, Mr Ellis. Mr Ellis will take you to the nurse. Carly, come with me. Everyone else. Out.

You wouldn't pick Carly and Gemma out as best friends in a line-up.

Gemma is a girly girl. She looks like she's fallen out of a rainbow and landed in Barbie's Jeep.

Carly just wears all her brother's hand-me-downs.

She's had a hard time. She's covered in self-harm scars.

She never really smiled but she had this expression like she was just about to. The side of her mouth twitched and her eyebrows raised just a fraction higher than they should. It was so satisfying when she laughed, even if it was at me.

She's always fighting. I've caught her in a brawl with a wall before.

She banged her head against it. She looked so peaceful and sleepy afterwards and I told her I understood why she did it but I didn't want her to do it again and she gave me a hug.

I never reported that.

After that particular fight Carly and I walked to the mound opposite school.

> MISS *sits down with* CARLY. MISS *waits.*

MISS Do you want to tell me what happened, Carly? *(beat)* We're not going anywhere until you tell me what's going on.

I can sit here all day.

Hmmm... Oh dear.

This is going to really drag, isn't it?

CARLY *(huffing)* Fine.

They always spill eventually.

Gemma started it this time. Apparently. She thought Carly was flirting with some boy she fancies.

MISS You know you can talk to me about boys.

CARLY Eww, Miss. No.

MISS Or if you are...you know? Having...[sex] If there is a boy you like and you might...Take it to the next – umm... Because the boys' school, I know they can all be a bit – I don't know. Keen.

CARLY Miss. You're really bad at this.

MISS I'm just saying I have ears and they can be rented out. For free obviously.

CARLY Seriously, Miss?

MISS Remember the song from PSHE?

CARLY No, please, Miss. Not your song.

MISS "Hey, what's up? Wrap it up. Or you ain't getting none of this."

CARLY Oh my God, Miss!

MISS I just want you to know you can talk to me.

CARLY I know I can, Miss.

MISS Good. Great! Yay.

CARLY Calm down. Can I go now?

I know you shouldn't have favourites but...

You always end up loving the troublemakers and the fuck-ups because you spend so much time with them in detention.

Carly and I played games to make the time go faster. Once, I bet her that she couldn't clean the locker room in under three minutes. She did it in two fifty-nine.

I'd promised her a prize so I raided the staff room but all I could find was:

CARLY A rich tea biscuit, that's a shit prize. At least get me a custard cream.

MISS Carly. It's the thought that counts.

That's what gave me the idea to do the Grand National registration.

They all put a pound in and picked a horse and the Monday after the race everyone was laughing because I'd picked a horse called Passing Wind who had tripped over his own hoof.

And at the end of registration I went to find Carly because she wasn't there.

I checked the timetable and she didn't have Maths. That's when she usually skives.

I came to the bench on the mound. Sometimes she sits and smokes in plain view when she's skiving. Like she wants me to find her. But she wasn't here that day.

At lunch, Mr Butterman came into the canteen. His face was redder than usual and his voice was low. He asked me to come with him.

He took me into his office, sat me down on the red sofa, gave me a box of tissues and he told me.

I remember very little from that time. Only that it was very silent. In the corridors, in class, in the canteen.

When a student dies...

It's everywhere.

It's been two months now. They've given me some time off. To – I guess to process or – I don't know when I'm going back but...

So, anyway, after my teenage strop last night I thought I'd better go to the corner shop and buy stuff for the house.

Loo roll, kitchen roll, sausage roll. Bin bags, bleach, box of raisins.

Ding-a-ling. Shop door opens.

MISS Can I get some menthol cigarettes please?

RAJ Sure. You want the neck lumps or the sleeping man?

MISS I think he might be the dead man.

RAJ Oh, right. God. Ok. Neck lumps it is.

A young guy in an red Adidas jacket.

He smelt nice, like hazelnuts. He smiled at me and I did a smile that I hoped looked like I hadn't just been smelling him.

He scanned the cigarettes.

MISS I've not smelt you in here before. I mean, seen you.
Normally there's an older guy.

RAJ My uncle! He's letting me stay so I work a few shifts. I'm
doing my masters – English Literature.

MISS No way! I teach English Lit and Creative Writing at
Lincoln Hill. Well, I'm on a bit of a break.

RAJ You're a teacher! Yeah. You look like a teacher. I think it's
the cardigan. I'm Raj, by the way.

**He was quite good-looking in a kind of accidental way. Like
a handsome man who's been given an electric shock.**

He gave me my change.

I haven't really fancied anyone for a while. Not since...

**I left the shop and got on the train to Guildford to get the
tree and –**

The train doors open.

Wet Warren got into the same carriage.

LAURA Oh, hi. Hiyeee! Hello! Oh, look at you.

(*to a woman next to* MISS) Excuse me, can I sit next to my
friend, please? Thank you.

Aww. Oh. Urgh. You seem, I don't know. Sad.

**She started to cry at me. I was annoyed but was quietly happy
it was her and not me.**

Are *you* ok? Mairead said that you've been staying in a lot.
I'm glad to see you out and about.

Shall I teach you a quick Kundalini meditation?

MISS I'm fine. Thank you.

LAURA Oh, come on. I do it all the time, just as a preventative
so I don't get to where you are.

I just don't want you to feel sad.

MISS I'm not sad.

LAURA You seem really really sad.

Shall we book in some sessions?

Not seeing Wet Warren is the only good thing about being off school. She used to hang around us like a bad smell.

The night that Mairead took me out to get over Seb, she invited herself and kept banging on about how loud music gives her tummy aches.

Mairead and I had finished early and got ready in the staffroom. I was a bit stressed because of Seb and Carly and Gemma's fight, but Mairead was so excited.

MAIREAD I'm so happy you are coming out!

It's like when KitKat Chunky bring out a new flavour like peanut butter or whatever and you think, oh, I think I'm gonna like that, and then you buy it and you try it and you LOVE it!

D'you get me?

MISS Not really, no.

Then at the end-of-day bell, Jack Ellis came in.

MAIREAD What is that smell? Can you smell that? Smells like a rebound.

Look at him. In his little smart shirt. He's coming out for you. He never comes out!

MISS I'm not really in the mood. I keep thinking about Seb.

MAIREAD Right. You know what he is. He's a pickle. A little fucking pickle in a jar. He used to be a juicy cucumber, sure. But he was a dick and now he's old and pickled and he's just going to give you a fucking stomach ache.

MISS What are you talking about?

MAIREAD You need to get that pickle out and either you do that by smashing the jar against a wall or getting a fork and letting me help you get laid. Do you get me?

MISS No.

MAIREAD All I'm saying is you don't want to spend the rest of your life fishing around for a shit pickle in a jar full of acid brine. Jack is coming over. Good luck!

MISS Mairead!

Jack came up and told me he was coming out and that I looked nice and my whole body went numb.

MR ELLIS There's some of that wine from parents' evening left in the fridge. You want a glass of that?

MISS Yes please. I love parents' evening...and wine.

> **MR ELLIS** *laughs.*

You had a haircut.

MR ELLIS I did. Well spotted. Yours is down. Looks nice.

MISS Thanks. I washed it. Recently.

MR ELLIS You up for a big one?

MISS Yes, I am up for a dance. Not with you though because you are dangerous.

MR ELLIS I actually am. I tried to do the Macarena at my sister's wedding and I knocked out my grandma.

MISS Really?

MR ELLIS No. Sorry. I'm trying to be funny but it's not working. You make me a bit nervous.

MISS It was funny.

MR ELLIS Sorry to hear about your fella.

MISS I didn't love him.

MR ELLIS Ok. Well, he's an idiot. You're a catch and he is an idiot.

MISS Thanks. How about you? Any romance?

MR ELLIS Sadly no. Can't get on board with those apps. And
I don't know if "divorced, food tech teacher with terrible
dance moves" is a great tag line.

MISS I don't know. I think you'd clean up on those things.

**He blushed then and smiled at me but the moment was quickly
ruined because Mairead started miming fingering behind
his back.**

**I still think about it a lot. Which I hate. Wet Warren says
I have an obsessive personality. I don't need sessions with
her do I? When she tells me all this shit for free, in public.**

Earlier today, when we were on the train:

LAURA Oh, this is my stop.

You have to let yourself be sad because it's ok and if you
don't it can manifest in all sorts of illnesses.

The train doors beep.

My aunt got cancer because she never let herself cry.

You need to admit what you've—

The doors close and her head yanks backwards.

Oh my God. My ponytail. My ponytail is stuck in the doors.
Someone. Help!

The train starts to pull out of the station.

Pull the alarm!

Her eyes are bigger than her head.

A man in a suit says, "that girl's hair is caught in the door".

LAURA HELP ME! I'm going to lose my ponytail.

I can't stop laughing.

LAURA Why are you laughing? My ponytail.

TANNOY "THE NEXT STATION IS LONDON ROAD GUILDFORD."

LAURA Ahhhh!

The train doors open.

Her hair was released.

LAURA *cradles her ponytail, relieved.*

LAURA That was so scary.

She gets off the train. The doors beep again.

So.

She puts her arm inside the train door holding it open.

What I was saying was, if you don't admit that you've – ah! My bag! My bag!

LAURA *jumps out as the doors close. Screaming.*

Karma is a babe!

I got off the train at Guildford and went to get my results.

I mean the tree.

I did get tested after Seb and didn't have chlamydia so it must have been a dirty towel after all.

I got an enduring oak.

It came up on the suggestions from my questionnaire answers – it's all done through an app.

It was only small, about up to my hip, but the woman assured me that it would grow quickly.

I decided to come straight to Lincoln Hill and show Mr Butterman the tree before he went home from school.

I sat here on the mound with my enduring oak, watching the kids and teachers leaving.

I miss it.

I watched Gemma walk out the school gates and unlock her
bike.

I thought she saw me so I waved.

But she got on her bike and rode off.

Probably didn't recognise me. I'm quite far away.

Imagine losing your best friend at sixteen.

I left the mound and went to the corner shop to buy a bottle
of wine. Not because I wanted to see Raj. But when I did see
him it was nice and I had a little vision of us holding hands
and skipping through a park.

He laughed at me for buying the cheap stuff. It's the crap that
Jack and I were drinking before we went out to Coochie's.
It tastes like lighter fluid but it does the trick.

Coochie's is the only club or bar that stays open past midnight
in Guildford.

I'm not much of a clubber. I've only been to Coochie's a
handful of times, one of them being the post-Seb, potential-
Jack evening.

MAIREAD This is fucking great! Look at all the hot guys in here.
It's like the man who runs the candy shop has not only left
the key in the lock but the wind has blown all the candy
right into my open mouth. Do you get me? Mr Jack Ellis
is staring a hole through your head right now.

MISS No, he isn't. Is he? I don't know how to do this.

MAIREAD This is what alcohol is for! Confidence is found in
tequila!

I'm ready to pounce on the guy from the stag dressed as a
Ninja Turtle.

Ah ha! *(to barman)* We would like four tequilas, a Stella
for me and –

MISS I'm gonna have a prosecco. Don't want to get too drunk.

Music changes. MISS *dances. Very drunk.* MISS *does a tequila shot. She dances with her drink.*

She starts doing the dance she taught her form.

Jack was standing at the edge of the dance floor.

MR ELLIS So it was you who taught them that dance!

I remember really dancing. Not-care dancing. Feeling sexy. A bit. A bit sexy. Not silly anyway.

He danced towards me, joking but serious too. Serious about me. About dancing with me.

Mr Ellis. *Fit Mr Ellis.*

The man of the school's dreams. Dancing with me. In the middle.

His hands were so big and he smelt amazing. Like man. Woody chocolate-y yum.

And he spun me round and kissed me. And the room span. From drinking and from the romance of the moment too. He tasted like coffee and cigarettes and I imagined us for that moment being a couple, kissing in our living room, in the morning, after coffee and his cigarette. I remember thinking, "don't ruin this".

And my heart was fast and my feet weren't really working anymore, I couldn't feel my legs. Only my lips. This is what it feels like. I thought. When someone really likes you.

It seems odd to me now. How much fun I was having in that moment. How happy I felt.

I sometimes wish... [I could cancel things out of my memory.]

When Mr Butterman came out of school today, I was waiting outside with the oak.

I ran over and told him about the woman in the shop and how the tree is perfect.

MISS Where shall we plant it? Can we do it now? Or shall we wait until, I don't know, maybe a ceremony or...

He put his big arm around me and led me behind his car.

MR BUTTERMAN It's a lovely tree, a lovely idea. But...now is not the right time.

MISS Well, when then?

MR BUTTERMAN Let's think about it.

I was holding the oak so hard that my hand was bleeding a bit. He opened his car door.

MR BUTTERMAN Look, I know you want to come back but whilst you're still feeling like this, I think it's best if you keep away from school. For some of the kids it's just...a bit much.

MISS But we need to do something to remember her.

MR BUTTERMAN Please, think some more about talking to someone.

He closed the tiny door of his Smart car.

Stupid car.

I'm not trying to come back, I'm trying to plant a tree.

I watched his car drive away.

I sat then, drank the wine from Raj's shop and smoked my menthols, looking into his office. You can see his red sofa. I can imagine sitting there. Sitting on that sofa. I can hear him saying it.

She'd locked herself in the bathroom.

Her mother had got in and found her. Seen her – like that. I have it in my head. I keep imagining it.

I guess I haven't really... [been dealing with it]

I can't be here.

I'm going to take my tree and go to a bar.

A Hawaiian bar.

I order a piña colada and do an Instagram story that makes it look like I'm on holiday in Hawaii. I have twenty-two followers now and three of them are strangers!

Fine. I won't come back to school. I'll just stay in Hawaii.

Text sound.

Mairead's onto me.

I delete her texts and go on Tinder for a bit.

I try to order my third piña colada but apparently I've had enough. Too drunk for a piña colada. It's basically just MILK!

People love telling me what I want and think at the moment.

How kind of them. So nice to have a rest from using my own brain. Thank you so so much.

I message everyone I've ever matched with on Tinder asking if they're out. I even message Seb. And stalk his Instagram.

I know I shouldn't – I don't want to sleep with anyone. I haven't since Jack.

Mairead had gone home with the Ninja Turtle from the stag do and we'd been dancing and drinking so many tequilas.

I was so drunk I left the dance floor to sit in a booth because I was feeling sick.

There was a girl next to me in the booth, and I feel like she was laughing at me.

Jack came over. Asked if I was ok. Said he'd take me home.

The next thing I remember we were in the loos.

He was holding my face and telling me to stay with him.

When I woke up he was gone. My skirt and bra were still on but my top was up by my neck and my pants weren't on. I found them down by the side of the loo.

I could feel what had happened.

When I got home I knocked on Mairead's bedroom door but she wasn't in.

When she got back she asked if we'd slept together and I just said yes. I didn't know how to tell her it hadn't been... I wasn't.

Maybe I am quite drunk.

I don't know... [what to do]

I don't want to go home. I need to get... [some help]. I need to get some more cigarettes.

Ding-a-ling. Shop door.

RAJ You're drunk.

MISS You are.

RAJ Nice tree. I'm more used to flowers as a gift but a tree is –

MISS /Get off it.

He gives me some water from the fridge. I reach behind the till and help myself to some little tiny vodkas.

He grills me like a detective and I tell him it's a memorial tree and do impressions of him as though he has an eye glass.

MISS Oh, hello, I'm Detective Raj, memorial tree must mean a murderrr!

RAJ Look, maybe I should get you a cab home, you seem a little too drunk.

MISS Oh, shut up. It's not embarrassing. I'm young.

She trips over.

He steadies me and I explain that Carly is like an enduring oak and she will live forever inside the tree. I ask him if he's ever met a girl who carries a tree and talks about death before.

RAJ I used to date a goth so yeah. We talked about sacrificing mice and what happens after you die. I know. Sexy.

I manage a laugh but I can barely hear him. I'm concentrating on downing my vodkas.

He talks and talks about death and books and poetry and I'm talking too but not really, just agreeing and thinking.

RAJ It's comforting to believe that there is a life after death. For me.

MISS I hope so. I hope everyone who's dead is happy. Except for horrible people.

RAJ So you hope that heaven and hell exist.

MISS Yeah. But I don't wanna think about the admin.

RAJ I'm imagining there is a little court up there where you plead your case.

MISS Well, I think I'll settle out of court. Straight to hell.

RAJ No, you won't.

MISS Yep, I'm a liar.

RAJ Everyone lies.

MISS When I lie people die.

RAJ You're very dramatic.

MISS Don't laugh at me.

RAJ Sorry. I'm sorry. Don't cry. We can just sit for a bit. We don't have to talk.

He's just looking at me. Watching me. My eyes won't stop.

He's looking and looking and taking me in. He shuffles himself towards me. He's flushed and he's breathing funny.

He puts his arm around my shoulder – I push him off and run away. Perv. He's shouting after me, something about trying to help. Trying to help me.

Loud music thumps. MISS *does a shot.*

I'm in Coochie's. With Carly's tree. I haven't been back since that night.

There is a handsome man at the end of the bar watching me dance. He's nodding at me.

Calling me over.

He's wearing a suit. Got a real Clark Kent thing about him. Boring at first glance but on the second it's clear he has a secret identity.

He's pointing at the door and waving.

I sexy slide towards him.

MISS Hi.

What?

I can't hear you – so loud in here.

Huh?

This is so silly. Huh?

Come here.

I pull him in to my ear and he shouts.

SUIT MAN I'm sorry, I was actually looking at the girl behind you.

MISS Ok. Cool. See you later.

I won't see you later.

So stupid.

Music thumps muffled by the toilet.

I hide in the loos. The same loos. It's the same toilet attendant that let me out that night. She doesn't recognise me.

She's staring at me, rattling her little tip plate. A shell with old pound coins on it. Not a good night for her either.

CRYSTAL Lolly? Hair grip? Spray?

MISS Spray. Please. Oh, wow. That is an interesting smell. Strong. Lovely, thank you.

CRYSTAL £3.

MISS What? What did you say?

£3? £3? For a tiny spritz? You sprayed it before you told me. What am I supposed to wash it off? I'm not paying three fucking pounds for –

She hits the tip plate out of CRYSTAL's *hand. The coins scatter.*

I – sorry. It's not the spray. It's...

She remembers me then.

I shouldn't have come back here.

I run away before she could say anything.

I've thought a lot about the Monday after that night with Jack.

He came into the staffroom and offered me a cup of tea.

He was just the same.

I was worried that I had remembered it wrong.

I did a pregnancy test that lunch. I convinced myself that if I was pregnant I would have to tell someone. So I did know.

It was negative.

I had a meeting with Mr Butterman about Carly and Gemma's fight and he said I seemed distracted. He asked me if I was ok and I said I was fine which was a lie. I could have said something then.

Mairead made a comment about how cool it was that we were so casual about getting together at the weekend – something about it being a true rebound. And I remember feeling really pleased that I seemed casual. I knew she'd be horrified if I told her but I just –

Ding-dong. MISS *rings the bell.*

Can't find my keys.

MISS   Hellooooo! Ding-dong. It's me!

Mairead opens the door. So serious. You can see how old she is when she doesn't smile.

I walk past her and head for the fridge.

MAIREAD   Can I get you a knife for that cheese? No, you are just gonna go for it. Good for you.

I was worried about you. Where have you been?

Tell me what's going on?

MISS How old are you? Hmmm? Why don't you tell me *that*?

MAIREAD Right, this needs to stop. You are losing it. Kim said
you came to school today. Chasing him around with a tree.

I—

I've lost the tree.

Carly. I've lost her tree.

I go to Coochie's, nothing. The Hawaiian bar, nothing. Outside
school.

Nothing.

Of course I've lost it. Of course I have. Can't look after
anything or anyone.

I need to find something. Anything. Anything to remember
her.

She searches for a tree and digs up a weed..

Back at the flat, Wet Warren is sitting in our kitchen. Her
face smug, her head tilted.

MISS Why is she in our house?

LAURA I was worried. Mr Butterman told us about the tree
and then Mairead rang and said you'd run off.

MISS Laura, go away.

LAURA Stop it. Stop telling me to go away. I'm just trying
to help. You need to talk about all this. You can't blame
yourself, it's not your fault.

She knows it's my fault. The very fact that she said it means
she knows it's my fault.

Gemma told me the day after she died. She stayed back after
registration and I held her hand whilst she cried and I tried
hard not to cry myself so that at least one of us wasn't.

GEMMA It's so shit, Miss.

MISS I know. *(beat)* Gemma, you know you can talk to me, don't you?

GEMMA I know I can, Miss. I wish I could say sorry.

MISS I know, but it's not your fault. You know that, don't you?

GEMMA It was – you know how she gets. She was – I don't want to get anyone in trouble.

MISS Gemma, you are being so brave, you aren't in trouble.

GEMMA I was – you know were were fighting because – I fancied…someone and he started flirting with her and saying she was beautiful and – in front of me – and everyone was noticing. And he was really keen on her so everyone was teasing her, calling her names on Insta and stuff. And she was saying she didn't like him and she was upset 'cos I was joining in.

And then she told me that she'd been kissing him and texting him and I was so angry and I wasn't talking to her.

I wasn't really sure I believed her. But then they had sex and she said that she didn't really want to.

MISS Who is this boy?

GEMMA It was at school.

And then she told me.

Mr Ellis. Jack.

He'd done it to her when she was in detention. When he was meant to be supervising.

He must have been able to sense how vulnerable she was. How much she needed someone.

I took Gemma to Mr Butterman. She told him.

Mr Butterman was distraught. He made some calls and sent everyone home for the day. Mr Ellis was arrested.

And that was it.

I could've... [said something and this wouldn't have happened]

I told Mr Butterman what he had done to me then.

I know. I know it was... [too late]

Mairead and Laura have cornered me in the kitchen.

LAURA Please let me help you, I know how sad you are.

MISS Look, Laura, I don't know why you stand to make me feel shit about myself every time you see me.

Did it ever occur to you that if you feel sad, you don't want some smug streak of a woman pointing right at you and telling you she can tell?

I have to live with the fact that things could have been different.

It is my fault.

I could have had the courage to tell someone straight away that he took me into a toilet and fucked me when I was too drunk to see and then maybe – maybe Carly would still be here.

I would do anything to bring her back. Anything.

So yes, Laura, I am sad. I am sad. I am fucking sad.

Now get out of my house.

Carly used to always forget to give me a present at the end of term. It's a thing the girls do, a tradition. And Carly never remembered.

And last year when everyone was giving me what their parents had bought me she walked up to my desk with a little piece of paper. It was a corner of lined paper she'd ripped out of her work book and it just said, "it's the thought that counts".

I felt awful that I liked it so much more than any of the candles or the vouchers but I couldn't help it.

She just never gave anything away, so if she gave you the slightest hint it was everything.

I knew how much she was. How much she had. How could I ever forget that.

Beat.

Mairead knocked on my door twice last night but I didn't let her in. I woke up this morning to find a note asking me to meet her on the mound opposite school.

She's walking towards me.

She sits next to me and we both stare at the school.

We don't say anything for a long time.

MAIREAD Seeing as you stole it so gallantly from the park, I thought we could plant this memorial weed.

She gets up and begins to dig.

MAIREAD I know you can't see this right now but it's going to be ok.

It's not your fault. None of this is ever your fault, these are different things it's like – it's like one of your pasta medleys. You can't mix spaghetti with fusilli. I mean how are you meant to eat it? What cutlery do you use? A spoon? A fork? Chopsticks?

Those two pastas should not be in the same bowl. What I'm saying is that if you can't see that, you need to get the pizza. Do you get me?

MISS Not really, no.

MAIREAD Ok, it's like a pickle. A little fucking pickle in a jar...

MISS You've already done this one.

MAIREAD What? No I haven't...

MISS Yes, you have. It's like a pickle, a pickle I've let rot inside me getting worse and now I'm trying to get rid of it by smashing the jar against the wall and fishing around in the brine when I should be talking about it and asking someone to help me.

MAIREAD No, I can't have said that. Makes far too much sense.

I'll leave you to it.

She hands me a brown paper tag and a pen. I watch her walk down the mound back to school. Breaktime's over and it's quiet.

I write Carly a note.

I'm sorry.

She takes a packet of raisins out of her pocket. She takes out a raisin. Holds it between her fingers. Smells it. Rolls it around on her lips. Puts it in her mouth, closes her eyes – chokes.

Blackout.

THIS IS NOT THE END

Visit samuelfrench.co.uk and discover the best theatre bookshop on the internet.

A vast range of plays
Acting and theatre books
Gifts

Lightning Source UK Ltd.
Milton Keynes UK
UKHW02f1955310718

326572UK00008B/205/P